GW00649757

November 1993

To Lucas
with much love,
Clorenge

THE POLITICIAN'S QUOTATION BOOK

The Politician's Quotation Book

A Literary Companion

Edited by
GYLES BRANDRETH, MP

ROBERT HALE · LONDON

ISBN 0 7090 5127 1

Robert Hale Limited
Clerkenwell House
Clerkenwell Green
London EC1R 0HT

Photoset in Goudy by
Derek Doyle & Associates, Mold, Clwyd.
Printed and bound in Hong Kong
by Bookbuilders Ltd.

Preface

Not long ago I had rather a tiring day. It began with a birthday breakfast at the Carlton Club (where at 8 a.m. an excellent claret was served with the devilled kidneys) and ended with supper with Richard Nixon. In between I managed morning coffee with the Princess of Wales, lunch with the Chancellor of the Exchequer (just home-made soup and sandwiches, you understand) and tea with a publisher. This is not a typical day (usually I do not bother with morning coffee), but it may help explain why some members of parliament seem a little remote from reality. We walk with kings, but not all of us keep the common touch.

Some of us do not even keep a diary. This is especially a nuisance when the publisher in question is offering you good money for 365 political *bons mots*, as long as at least ten per cent have not been seen in print before. The publisher is not producing a book (and certainly not this book), but a tear-off desk calendar which will feature a nugget of political wisdom for every day of the year. The task is more challenging than might at first appear because the space available beneath the date means that none of the political *aperçus* can run to more than twenty words. The publisher has sought me out at the House of Commons because he is convinced I am the man for the job.

Recognizing that a touch of self-deprecation may not go amiss, I mutter that, of course, I only became an MP in 1992. 'That doesn't matter,' booms my companion (whose tear-off desk calendar aimed at anglers sells over 100,000 copies a year), 'You must have been rubbing shoulders with the great and the good for years. All we need is a few of their best quips. Who was the first Prime Minister you met?'

'Harold Macmillan.'

'There you are. What did he say?'

'Not a lot.'

'What do you mean, not a lot?'

'Well, not anything, actually. I went to have tea with him when I was at Oxford and he slept soundly throughout.'

As we all know, the first Earl of Stockton said many memorable things. It's just unfortunate he said none of them to me.

'Forget Macmillan then. Who did you meet next? Churchill? Kennedy?'

'Diefenbaker.'

'Who?'

The calendar king (whose *Cats and Kittens Annual* is a best-seller on both sides of the Atlantic) has not heard of John Diefenbaker, the former Canadian Prime Minister. This is a pity because Diefenbaker certainly said something that rings a bell with a new member of parliament: 'For the first six months you will wonder how you ever got there. After that you will wonder how the rest of the members ever got there.'

Canadian Prime Ministers have a special way with words. I cherish particularly Pierre Trudeau's exchange with a member of the press corps on the campaign trail in 1968:

Newshound: Will you give up your Mercedes.
Trudeau: Are you talking of the car now, or the girl?
Newshound: The car.
Trudeau: I won't give up either.

Alas the calendar king does not want Canadians. He wants Britons or Americans. Most of all he wants Churchill. I offer Churchill's definition of political skill: 'The ability to foretell what is going to happen tomorrow, next week, next month and next year, and to have the ability afterwards to explain why it did not happen.' He likes it, but it is too long.

'I need them short and snappy, like Harold Wilson's "A week is a long time in politics." '

'Or,' I venture, 'Never apologize, never explain.'

'Perfect length. Who said it?'

I am not sure and I am still trying to find out. If you know, please get in touch. Some people say it is Benjamin Disraeli. Viscount Mersey tells me it is Benjamin Jowett, the celebrated Master of Balliol College, Oxford, who offered it as a maxim to Mersey's great-grandfather, Lord Lansdowne, around 1880. The editor of the *Penguin Dictionary of Quotations* attributes the phrase to Admiral Lord Fisher, First Sea Lord during the Great War. There is an intriguing variation of it in advice given by Stanley Baldwin and recorded by Harold Nicolson in 1943: 'You will find in politics that you are much exposed to the attribution of false motive. Never complain and never explain.'

Getting to the root of who said what and who said it first is not easy. Macmillan's famous 'Wind of Change' speech to the South African parliament in 1960 echoed Baldwin on India a generation before: 'There is a wind of nationalism and freedom blowing round the world.' In 1954 Churchill declared that 'Talking jaw to jaw is better than going to war.' Four years later Macmillan made it a line fit for desk diaries by recasting it as 'Jaw-jaw is better than war-war.'

Happily there are no rival claimants to Sir Alec Douglas-Home's endearing confession: 'There are two problems in my life. The political ones are insoluble and the economic ones are incomprehensible.' Perhaps Sir Alec took to heart the advice of Sir Henry Wotton (1568-1639): 'Tell the truth and so puzzle and confound your adversaries.'

By this stage in the discussion it has become clear to both the calendar king and me that I am not, after all, the man for the job. To ask a politician who once featured in the *Guinness Book of Records* for making a speech lasting twelve and a half hours to confine himself to political sound bites running to a maximum of twenty words is asking too much – or rather, too little. Amicably we go our separate ways, he in search of an alternative compiler for his calendar, I in search of a publisher who might be interested in a more leisurely, and perhaps slightly more literary, gallimaufry of political quotations. Happily I found him, and this little volume is the result.

While there may be a quotation here for every day of the year this does not aim to be a quick-fire collection of parliamentary put-downs and political one-liners. It is simply a personal anthology of observations, some ancient, some modern, some terse, some in verse, some familiar, some (I hope) surprising, on the art and craft of politics; observations that have caught my eye and, I trust, may please yours.

GYLES BRANDRETH MP

It is the highest and most legitimate pride of an Englishman to have the letters MP written after his name. No selection from the alphabet, no doctorship, no fellowship, be it of ever so learned or royal a society, no knightship, – not though it be of the Garter, – confers so fair an honour.

ANTHONY TROLLOPE
Can You Forgive Her?, 1864

To err is human. To blame someone else is politics.
   HUBERT HUMPHREY

Politics, n. A strife of interests masquerading as a contest of principles. The conduct of public affairs for private advantage.
   AMBROSE BIERCE
   The Devil's Dictionary

A certain nobleman advised me to turn my thoughts towards politics immediately. 'You cannot direct your attention that way too early in this country,' said the Duke; 'they are the proper career for a young man of ability and your station in life. That course is the most advantageous because it is a monopoly. A little success in that line goes far, since the number of competitors is limited; and of those who are admitted to the contest the greater part are altogether devoid of talent, or are too indolent to exert themselves; so many are excluded that of the few who are permitted to enter it is difficult to find any that are not utterly unfit for the ordinary service of the State.'
   PERCY BYSSHE SHELLEY

Practical politics consists in ignoring facts.
   HENRY ADAMS

Politics is the gentle art of getting votes from the poor and campaign funds from the rich, by promising to protect each other from the other.
OSCAR AMERINGER

Politics, it seems to me, for years, or all too long,
Has been concerned with right or left instead of right or wrong.
RICHARD ARMOUR

Politics is the art of looking for trouble, finding it whether it exists or not, diagnosing it incorrectly, and applying the wrong remedy.
SIR ERNEST BENN

Politics is a blood sport.
ANEURIN BEVAN

There is a holy mistaken zeal in politics as well as in religion. By persuading others we convince ourselves.
FRANCISCUS JUNIUS (1589-1677)

Politics is the art of the next best.
OTTO VON BISMARCK

Vain hope to make men happy by politics!
THOMAS CARLYLE
Journal, 1831

Politics are almost as exciting as war, and quite as dangerous. In war you can only be killed once, but in politics many times.
SIR WINSTON CHURCHILL

In politics nothing is contemptible.
>BENJAMIN DISRAELI
>*Vivian Grey*, 1827

In politics people like to give you what they think you deserve and deny you what they think you want.
>CECIL PARKINSON, 1992

Finality is not the language of politics.
>BENJAMIN DISRAELI, 1859

Politics is a deleterious profession, like some poisonous handicrafts.
>RALPH WALDO EMERSON

Politics is the art of the possible.
>R.A. BUTLER

Politics is not the art of the possible. It consists in choosing between the disastrous and the unpalatable.
>J.K. GALBRAITH

I have reached the conclusion that politics are too serious a matter to be left to the politicians.
>CHARLES DE GAULLE

Politics are now nothing more than a means of rising in the world.
>DR JOHNSON, 1775
>Boswell's *Life of Johnson*

Politics is a dog's life without a dog's decencies.
>RUDYARD KIPLING

Private passions grow tired and wear themselves out; political passions, never.
>   LAMARTINE

Politics, as the word is commonly understood, are nothing but corruptions.
>   PLATO

Politics is the art of preventing people from busying themselves with what is their own business.
>   PAUL VALÉRY

A week is a long time in politics.
>   HAROLD WILSON, 1964

In politics, if you want something said, ask a man; if you want anything done, ask a woman.
>   MARGARET THATCHER

Nothing is so admirable in politics as a short memory.
>   J.K. GALBRAITH

You will find in politics that you are much exposed to the attribution of false motive. Never complain and never explain.
>   STANLEY BALDWIN
>   quoted in Harold Nicolson's *Diaries*, 21 July 1943

Politics is perhaps the only profession for which no preparation is thought necessary.
>   ROBERT LOUIS STEVENSON
>   *Familiar Studies of Men and Books*, 1882

Politics are usually the executive expression of human immaturity.

VERA BRITTAIN, 1964

Politics and the fate of mankind are formed by men without ideals and without greatness. Those that have greatness within them do not go in for politics.

ALBERT CAMUS
Notebooks (1935-42)

In dealing with the State we ought to remember that its institutions are not aboriginal, though they existed before we were born; that they are not superior to the citizen; that every one of them was once the act of a single man; every law and usage was a man's expedient to meet a particular case; that they are all imitable, all alterable; we may make as good, we may make better.

RALPH WALDO EMERSON (1803-82)
'Politics'

They that govern most make least noise.
> JOHN SELDEN (1584-1654)
> *Table-talk*

I would not give half a guinea to live under one form of government rather than another. It is of no moment to the happiness of an individual.
> DR JOHNSON, 1772
> Boswell's *Life of Johnson*

That is the best government which desires to make the people happy, and knows how to make them happy.
> T.B. MACAULAY
> *On Mitford's History of Greece*, 1824

Were it left to me to decide, whether we should have a government without newspapers, or newspapers without a government, I should not hesitate a moment to prefer the latter.
> THOMAS JEFFERSON, 1787

Thomas
Jefferson

The worst thing in the world, next to anarchy, is government.
HENRY WARD BEECHER

Government is a contrivance of human wisdom to provide for human wants.
EDMUND BURKE

Nothing appears more surprising to those who consider human affairs with a philosophical eye, than the easiness with which the many are governed by the few.
DAVID HUME
'First Principles of Government', *Essays*, 1742

As to political honesty, there is no such thing. 'Tis of little consequence what a politician believes; the important thing is how much he can make others believe; that is the true secret of government.
LORD BYRON

The only good government ... is a bad one in a hell of a fright.
JOYCE CAREY
The Horse's Mouth, 1944

Nothing's more dull and negligent
Than an old, lazy government,
That knows no interest of state,
But such as serves a present strait.
SAMUEL BUTLER
Miscellaneous Thoughts

Government is the only institution that can take a valuable commodity like paper, and make it worthless by applying ink.

> LUDWIG VAN MOSES

Gardener:
Go thou, and like an executioner
Cut off the heads of too fast-growing sprays
That look too lofty in our commonwealth.
All must be even in our government.
You thus employed, I will go root away
The noisome weeds which without profit suck
The soil's fertility from wholesome flowers.

First Man:
Why should we, in the compass of a pale,
Keep law and form and due proportion,
Showing us in a model our firm estate,
When our sea-walled garden, the whole land,
Is full of weeds, her fairest flowers choked up,
Her fruit trees all unpruned, her hedges ruined,
Her knots disordered, and her wholesome herbs
Swarming with caterpillars?

> WILLIAM SHAKESPEARE
> *Richard II*

The art of government is the organisation of idolatry.

> BERNARD SHAW

To govern mankind one must not overrate them.

> LORD CHESTERFIELD

Government is an association of men who do violence to the rest of us.
LEO TOLSTOY

If it is true that vice can never be done away with, the science of government consists of making it contribute to the public good.
MARQUIS DE VAUVENARGUES
Reflections and Maxims, 1746

There has never been a perfect government, because men have passions; and if they did not have passions, there would be no need for government.
VOLTAIRE
Politique et législation: Idées républicaines

The idea of a perfect and immortal commonwealth will always be found as chimerical as that of a perfect and immortal man.
DAVID HUME
History of Great Britain, 1754

In all political regulations, good cannot be complete, it can only be predominant.
DR JOHNSON
Journey to the Western Islands, 1775

Truth is the glue that holds governments together.
GERALD FORD, 1974

It has always been desirable to tell the truth, but seldom if ever necessary to tell the whole truth.

ARTHUR BALFOUR

Themistocles said, 'The Athenians govern the Greeks; I govern the Athenians; you, my wife, govern me; your son governs you.'

PLUTARCH
Life of Cato the Censor

Dinners have become a means of government, and the fates of nations are decided at a banquet.

BRILLAT-SAVARIN (1755-1826)

King Louis Philippe once said to me that he attributed the great success of the British nation in political life to their talking politics after dinner.

DISRAELI
in a speech on being made Rector of Glasgow University, 1873

In a troubled state save as much for your own as you can. A dog had been to market to buy a shoulder of mutton. coming home he met two dogs by the way that quarrelled with him. He laid down his shoulder of mutton and fell to fighting with one of them. In the meantime the other dog fell to eating his mutton. He, seeing that, left the dog he was fighting with, and fell upon him that was eating. Then the other dog fell to eat. When he perceived there was no remedy, but which of them soever he fought withal his mutton was in danger, he thought he would have as much of it as he could, and thereupon gave over fighting and fell to eating himself.

JOHN SELDEN (1584-1653)

Agreeing to something on principle means that you have absolutely no intention of putting it into practice.

OTTO VON BISMARCK

The best reason why Monarchy is a strong government is that it is intelligible government. The mass of mankind understand it, and they hardly anywhere in the world understand any other.

WALTER BAGEHOT
The English Constitution, 1867

The Crown is, according to the saying, the 'fountain of honour'; but the Treasury is the spring of business.

WALTER BAGEHOT
The English Constitution, 1867

A crown is merely a hat that lets the rain in.

FREDERICK II of Prussia, 1740

There is not a single crowned head in Europe whose talents or merits would entitle him to be elected a vestryman by the people of any parish in America.

THOMAS JEFFERSON
in a letter to George Washington, 2 May 1788

If there is to remain among us a sovereign, that sovereign, even though divested of political power, should be endowed with all that personal respect can give. If we wish ourselves to be high, we should treat that which is over us as high.

ANTHONY TROLLOPE
Thackeray

Everyone likes flattery; and when you come to Royalty you should lay it on with a trowel.

attributed to BENJAMIN DISRAELI, 1880

Aristocracy, n. Government by the best men. (In this sense the word is obsolete; so is that kind of government.)

AMBROSE BIERCE
The Devil's Dictionary

Republics come to an end through luxury; monarchies through poverty.

MONTESQUIEU (1684-1755)

They that are discontented under a monarchy call it tyranny, and they that are displeased with aristocracy call it oligarchy; so also, they which find themselves grieved under a democracy call it anarchy.

THOMAS HOBBES (1588-1679)

You violent politicians make more rout about royalty than it is worth. It is only the highest place, and somebody must fill it, no matter who: neither do the persons themselves think so much of it as you do. They are glad to get into privacy as much as they can; nor is it a sinecure. The late king, I have been told, used often to have to sign his name to papers, and do nothing else for three hours together, till his fingers fairly ached, and then he would take a walk in the garden, and come in to repeat the drudgery for three hours more.

JAMES NORTHCOTE (1746-1831)

We hold these truths to be self-evident, that all men are created equal, that they are endowed by their Creator with certain unalienable rights, that among these are life, liberty and the pursuit of happiness. That to secure these rights, governments are instituted among men, deriving their just powers from the consent of the governed. That whenever any form of government becomes destructive of these ends, it is the right of the people to alter or abolish it, and to institute a new government ...

American Declaration of Independence, 1776

Liberty means responsibility. That is why most men dread it.

>GEORGE BERNARD SHAW
>*Maxims for Revolutionists*, 1903

We are all agreed as to our own liberty; we should have as much of it as we can get; but we are not agreed as to the liberty of others; for in proportion as we take, others must lose.

>DR JOHNSON
>Boswell's *Life of Johnson*

I know not what course others may take; but as for me, give me liberty, or give me death!

>PATRICK HENRY
>in a speech to the Virginia House of Delegates, 23 March 1775

If any man ask me what a free government is, I answer that for any practical purposes, it is what the people think it so.

>EDMUND BURKE
>*A Letter to the Sheriffs of Bristol*, 1777

The love of liberty is the love of others, the love of power is the love of ourselves.

>WILLIAM HAZLITT
>*Political Essays*, 1819

O Liberty, what crimes are committed in your name.

>MME ROLAND (1754-93)
>uttered on her way to the scaffold during the French Revolution

O Freedom, what liberties are taken in thy name!
>DANIEL GEORGE
>*The Perpetual Pessimist*, 1961

How could a state be governed ... if every individual remained free to obey or not to obey the law according to his private opinions.
>THOMAS HOBBES
>*Leviathan*, 1651

If all mankind minus one were of one opinion, and only one person were of the contrary opinion, mankind would be no more justified in silencing that one person, than he, if he had the power, would be justified in silencing mankind.
>JOHN STUART MILL
>*On Liberty*, 1859

Liberty is the right to do whatever the law permits.
>MONTESQUIEU
>*De l'esprit des lois*, 1748

It is with government as with medicine, its only business is the choice of evils. Every law is an evil, for every law is an infraction of liberty.
>JEREMY BENTHAM
>*Principles of Legislation*, 1789

Laws cannot make people moral, yet the more moral the people the higher their laws.
>NANCY ASTOR
>in a speech in the House of Commons, 1924

Men should not know how their laws or sausages are made.
OTTO VON BISMARCK

Liberty, n: one of imagination's most precious possessions.
AMBROSE BIERCE
The Devil's Dictionary

From the beginning all were created equal by nature, slavery was introduced through the unjust oppression of worthless men, against the will of God; for if God had wanted to create slaves, he would surely have decided at the beginning of the world who was to be slave and master.
JOHN BALL
in a sermon at Blackheath during the Peasants'
Uprising, 1381

It is better that some should be happy than that none should be happy, which would be the case in a general state of equality.
DR JOHNSON, 1776
Boswell's *Life of Johnson*

So far is it from being true that men are naturally equal, that no two people can be half an hour together, but one shall acquire an evident superiority over the other.
DR JOHNSON

What makes equality such a difficult business is that we only want it with our superiors.
HENRY BECQUE
Querelles littéraires, 1890

Equality may perhaps be a right, but no power on earth can ever turn it into a fact.
> HONORÉ DE BALZAC
> *La Duchesse de Langeais*, 1834

That all men should be brothers is the dream of people who have no brothers.
> CHARLES CHINCHOLLES
> *Pensées de tout le monde*, 1880

Democracy is a government in the hands of men of low birth, no property and unskilled labour.
> ARISTOTLE

To one that advised him to set up a democracy in Sparta, 'Pray,' said Lycurgus, 'do you first set up a democracy in your own house.'
> recalled in Plutarch's *Apophthegms of Kings and Great Commanders*

Universal suffrage is the government of a house by its nursery.
> OTTO VON BISMARCK

Decision by majorities is as much an expedient as lighting by gas.
> WILLIAM GLADSTONE

Democracy means government by discussion but it is only effective if you can stop people talking.
> CLEMENT ATTLEE

The greatest happiness of the greatest number is the foundation of morals and legislation.

JEREMY BENTHAM

Democracy means government by the uneducated, while aristocracy means government by the badly educated.

G.K. CHESTERTON

Governments arise either out of the people or over the people.

THOMAS PAINE
The Rights of Man, 1791

Democratic contrivances are quarantine measures against that ancient plague, the lust for power: as such, they are very necessary and very boring.

NIETZSCHE

It has been said that Democracy is the worst form of government except all those other forms that have been tried from time to time.

SIR WINSTON CHURCHILL
in a speech in the House of Commons, 11 November 1947

That this nation, under God, shall have a new birth of freedom, and that government of the people, by the people, for the people, shall not perish from the earth.

ABRAHAM LINCOLN
Speech at Gettysberg, 1863

High hopes were once formed of democracy; but democracy means simply the bludgeoning of the people by the people for the people.
>OSCAR WILDE
>*The Soul of Man Under Socialism*

Democ'cy gives every man
A right to be his own oppressor.
>JAMES LOWELL (1819-91)
>*Biglow Papers*

You can fool all the people some of the time, and some of the people all the time, but you cannot fool all the people all the time.
>attributed to ABRAHAM LINCOLN
>in a speech at Clinton, 8 September 1858

You can fool too many of the people too much of the time.
>JAMES THURBER
>*The Thurber Carnival*, 1945

One fifth of the people are against everything all the time.
>ROBERT KENNEDY, 1964

There is only one sound argument for democracy, and that is the argument that it is a crime for any man to hold himself out as better than other men, and, above all, a most heinous offence for him to prove it.
>H.L. MENCKEN, 1920

What makes a nation great is not primarily its great men, but the stature of its innumerable mediocre ones.
JOSE ORTEGA Y GASSET (1883-1955)

To worship the people is to be worshipped.
SIR FRANCIS BACON
De Augmentis Scientiarum, 1623

The British people, being subject to fogs, require grave statesmen.
BENJAMIN DISRAELI

You can never have a revolution in order to establish a democracy. You must have a democracy in order to have a revolution.

>G.K. CHESTERTON
>*Tremendous Trifles*

He that goeth about to persuade a multitude, that they are not so well governed as they ought to be, shall never want attentive and favourable hearers.

>RICHARD HOOKER
>*Ecclesiastical Polity*, 1594

Season for Reform – *Not* when we are at war, for then all is hurry and confusion, and our minds are too heated and agitated to set about so serious an affair. *Not* when we are at peace, for then it would be madness to disturb the tranquillity of the nation.

>CHARLES PIGOTT
>*A Political Dictionary: explaining the True Meaning of Words*, 1795

Though I admire republican principles in theory, yet I am afraid the practice may be too perfect for human nature. We tried a republic last century and it failed. Let our enemies try next. I hate political experiments.

>DR JOHNSON

All revolutions invariably encourage bad characters and potential criminals. Traitors throw off the mask; they cannot contain themselves amidst the general confusion that seems to promise easy victims.

>DELACROIX
>*Journal*, 1860

Revolution, n. In politics, an abrupt change in the form of misgovernment. Revolutions are usually accompanied by a considerable effusion of blood, but are accounted worth it – this appraisement being made by beneficiaries whose blood had not the mischance to be shed.

> AMBROSE BIERCE
> *The Devil's Dictionary*

On the 5th November we began our Parliament, to which the King should have come in person, but refrained, through a practice but that morning discovered. The plot was to have blown up the King ... at one instant and blast to have ruined the whole estate and kingdom of England.

> SIR EDWARD HOBY
> in a letter to Sir Thomas Edmondes, 19 November
> 1605, on the discovery of the Gunpowder Plot

The healthy spirit of self-help created amongst working people would more than any other measure serve to raise them as a class, and this, not by pulling down others, but by levelling them up to a higher and still advancing standard of religion, intelligence and virtue.

> SAMUEL SMILES
> *Self-help*, 1859

Therefore a Prince, so long as he keeps his subjects united and loyal, ought not to mind the reproach of cruelty because with a few examples he will be more merciful than those who, through too much mercy, allow disorders to arise.

> NICCOLO MACHIAVELLI
> *The Prince*, 1513

It is a political error to practise deceit, if deceit is carried
too far.
> FREDERICK II of Prussia
> *Antimachiaeval*, 1740

It is a very easy thing to devise good laws; the difficulty is to
make them effective. The great mistake is that of looking
upon men as virtuous, or thinking that they can be made so
by laws; and consequently the greatest art of a politician is
to render vices serviceable to the cause of virtue.
> LORD BOLINGBROKE (1672-1751)

Men are more easily governed through their vices than
through their virtues.
> NAPOLEON
> *Maxims*

Parliament cannot be called together before the day
appointed for the prorogation, unless under particular
circumstances. This is regulated by act of parliament.
When I was in office, we wished that Parliament should
meet before the day fixed by the prorogation. We felt great
difficulty about it. I explained the law to the cabinet, and
told them that unless there were some strong ground for it,
such as a disturbance or riot of the people, it could not be
done. 'Oh,' said Henry Dundas, afterwards Lord – – – – (I
forget his name, but never mind that), 'if that's all, I can
soon get up a very pretty riot in Scotland.'
> LORD ELDON (1751-1838)

Tell the truth, and so puzzle and confound your adversaries.
> SIR HENRY WOTTON (1568-1639)

In statesmanship get the formalities right, never mind
about the moralities.
> MARK TWAIN
> *Notebooks*

Political skill ... the ability to foretell what is going to
happen tomorrow, next week, next month and next year.
And to have the ability afterwards to explain why it did not
happen.
> SIR WINSTON CHURCHILL

Political necessities sometimes turn out to be political
mistakes.
> BERNARD SHAW
> *St Joan*, 1923

The constitution says that no man shall be taxed but by his
own consent: a very plausible theory, gentleman, but not
reducible to practice. Who will apply a lancet to his own
arm, and bleed himself? Very few, you acknowledge. Who
then, *a fortiori*, would apply a lancet to his own pocket, and
draw off what is dearer to him than his blood – his money?
Fewer still, of course: I humbly opine, none. – What then
remains but to apply a royal college of state surgeons, who
may operate on the patient according to their views of his
case? Taxation is a political phlebotomy: the Honourable
House is, figuratively speaking, a royal college of state
surgeons. A good surgeon must have firm nerves and a
steady hand; and, perhaps, the less feeling the better. Now,
it is manifest, that, as all feeling is founded on sympathy,
the fewer constituents a representative has, the less must be
his sympathy with the public, and the less, of course as is

desirable, his feeling for his patient – the people: – who, therefore, with so much *sang froid*, can phlebotomize the nation, as the representative of half an elector?

THOMAS LOVE PEACOCK
Melincourt, 1817

There is no art which one government sooner learns of another than that of draining money from the pockets of the people.

ADAM SMITH (1723-90)

The promises of yesterday are the taxes of today.
MACKENZIE KING, Canadian Prime Minister, 1931

Men, who prefer any load of infamy, however great, to any pressure of taxation, however light.
>   SYDNEY SMITH
>   *On American Debts*

What Englishman will give his mind to politics as long as he can afford to keep a motor car?
>   BERNARD SHAW
>   *The Apple Cart*, 1931

The Hon. Member for King's Lynn was good enough to suggest that we should tax diamonds, pearls, feathers and lace in a way which made me doubt whether he sufficiently realized that two of the highest and holiest feelings in woman's nature are the love of diamonds and the love of smuggling.
>   SIR MICHAEL HICKS BEACH, Chancellor of the
>   Exchequer
>   in a speech in the House of Commons, 19 March
>   1900

There are many golden rules in politics. Never believe a Chancellor who says he will never devalue. Never turn your back on a Tory whip. Never trust a politician who bleats about compassion – he merely wants to take money off you, give it to someone else and claim credit for his 'generosity'.
>   ANDREW ALEXANDER
>   *Daily Mail*, 16 October 1992

Administration, n. An ingenious abstraction in politics, designed to receive the kicks and cuffs due to the premier or president.
> AMBROSE BIERCE
> *The Devil's Dictionary*

O, that estates, degrees, and offices
Were not derived corruptly, and that clear honour
Were purchased by the merit of the wearer!
> WILLIAM SHAKESPEARE
> *King Lear*

A man destined to sit conspicuously on our Treasury bench, or on a seat opposite, should ask the Gods for a thick skin as a first gift.
> ANTHONY TROLLOPE
> *Phineas Redux*, 1876

All the armed prophets conquered, all the unarmed ones perished.

> NICCOLO MACHIAVELLI
> *The Prince*, 1513

Politics, as a practice, whatever its professions, has always been the systematic organisation of hatred.

> HENRY ADAMS
> *The Education of Henry Adams*, 1906

Only one more indispensable massacre of Capitalists or Communists or Fascists or Christians or Heretics, and there we are – there we are in the golden future.

> ALDOUS HUXLEY
> *Time Must Have a Stop*, 1944

The public weal requires that men should betray, and lie, and massacre.
> MONTAIGNE
> 'Of Profit and Honesty', *Essays* 1580-88

Never believe in anything until it has been officially denied.
> OTTO VON BISMARCK

Amongst those who dislike oppression are many who like to oppress.
> NAPOLEON
> *Maxims*

Unlimited power is apt to corrupt the minds of those who possess it; and this I know, my Lords, that where law ends, tyranny begins.
> WILLIAM PITT, Earl of Chatham
> in a speech in the House of Lords, 1770

All political power is a trust.
> CHARLES JAMES FOX

Necessity is the plea for every infringement of human freedom. It is the argument of tyrants; it is the creed of slaves.
> WILLIAM PITT THE YOUNGER
> in a speech in the House of Commons, 1783

In matters of government justice means force as well as virtue.
> NAPOLEON
> *Maxims*

The 'people' who exercise the power are not always the same people over whom it is exercised.
JOHN STUART MILL
On Liberty, 1859

Every despotism has a specially keen and hostile instinct for whatever keeps up human dignity and independence.
HENRI AMIEL
Journal intime, 1852

Power will intoxicate the best hearts, as wine the strongest heads.
CHARLES CALEB COLTON
Lacon, 1825

Power tends to corrupt, and absolute power corrupts absolutely. Great men are almost always bad men, even when they exercise influence and not authority. There is no worse heresy than that the office sanctifies the holder of it.
LORD ACTON
in a letter to Bishop Mandell Creighton, 3 April 1887

Power does not corrupt men; fools, however, if they get into a position of power, corrupt power.
BERNARD SHAW

Power worship blurs political judgment because it leads, almost unavoidably, to the belief that present trends will continue. Whoever is winning at the moment will always seem to be invincible.
GEORGE ORWELL
James Burnham and the Managerial Revolution, 1946

Diplomacy, n. The patriotic art of lying for one's country.
>AMBROSE BIERCE
>*The Devil's Dictionary*

Patriotism is the last refuge of a scoundrel.
>DR JOHNSON

Nobody, not even the most malevolently sceptical of democrats, would believe what charlatanry and pomposity there is in this diplomacy.
>OTTO VON BISMARCK
>in a letter to his wife, 18 May 1851

At bottom, every state regards another as a gang of robbers who will fall upon it as soon as there is an opportunity.
>ARTUR SCHOPENHAUER
>'On Jurisprudence and Politics', *Parerga and Paralipomena*, 1851

Talking of patriotism, what humbug it is; it is a word which always commemorates a robbery. There isn't a foot of land in the world which doesn't represent the ousting and re-ousting of a long line of successive owners.
>MARK TWAIN
>*A Connecticut Yankee at King Arthur's Court*, 1889

English policy is to float lazily downstream, occasionally putting out a diplomatic boat-hook to avoid collisions.
>LORD SALISBURY (1830-1903)

We seem, as it were, to have conquered and peopled half the world in a fit of absence of mind.

> SIR JOHN SEELEY
> *The Expansion of England*, 1883

If we were to do for ourselves what we have done for our country, we should indeed be very great rogues.

> CAMILIO CAVOUR, first Prime Minister of a united
> Italy, 1860

A nation is only at peace when it's at war.

> HUGH KINGSMILL

Jaw-jaw is better than war-war.

> HAROLD MACMILLAN, 1958

All the business of war, and indeed all the business of life, is an endeavour to find out what you don't know by what you do; that's what I called 'guessing what was at the other side of the hill'.

> DUKE OF WELLINGTON, 1852

A healthy nation is as unconscious of its nationality as a healthy man of his bones. But if you break a nation's nationality it will think of nothing else but getting it set again.

> BERNARD SHAW
> Preface to *John Bull's Other Island*, 1904

How is the world ruled and how do wars start? Diplomats tell lies to journalists and then believe what they read.

> KARL KRAUS
> *Aphorisms and More Aphorisms*, 1909

But Europe is not to be saved by the exertions of any single man. England has saved herself by her exertions, and will, as I trust, save Europe by her example.

> WILLIAM PITT THE YOUNGER
> in a speech at the Guildhall, 1805

Hope nothing from foreign governments. They will never be really willing to aid you until you have shown that you are strong enough to conquer without them.

> MAZZINI
> *Young Italy*

What experience and history teach is this – that people and governments never have learned anything from history, or acted on the principles deduced from it.

> G.W.F. HEGEL (1770-1831)
> *The Philosophy of History*

World History. It's just the study of a succession of human follies and nothing more. The only subjects I respect are mathematics and the natural sciences.

> DOSTOEVSKY
> *The Brothers Karamazov*, 1880

A horrible voice, bad breath and a vulgar manner – the characteristics of a popular politician.

> ARISTOPHANES
> 5th century BC

Politicians neither love nor hate. Interest, not sentiment, governs them.

> LORD CHESTERFIELD (1694-1763)

Politician, n. An eel in the fundamental mud upon which the superstructure of organized society is reared. As compared with the statesman, he suffers the disadvantage of being alive.

> AMBROSE BIERCE
> *The Devil's Dictionary*

The most successful politician is he who says what the people are thinking most often in the loudest voice.

> THEODORE ROOSEVELT, 26th President of the USA
> (1858-1919)

This might be the pate of a politician, which this ass now o'erreaches; one that would circumvent God, might it not?

> WILLIAM SHAKESPEARE
> *Hamlet* (grave-digger's scene)

    Get thee glass eyes;
  And, like a scurvy politician, seem
  To see the things thou dost not.
    WILLIAM SHAKESPEARE
    King Lear

It is as hard and severe a thing to be a true politician as to be truly moral.
    FRANCIS BACON
    Advancement of Learning, 1605

No man can be a Politician, except he be first an Historian or a Traveller; (for except he can see what Must be, or what May be, he is no politician).
    JAMES HARRINGTON
    The Commonwealth of Oceana, 1656

We both went into office early, and the anxiety to do special duties well probably deterred us both from thinking much of the great question. When a man has to be on the alert to keep Ireland quiet, or to prevent peculation in the dockyards, or to raise the revenue while he lowers the taxes, he feels himself to be saved from the necessity of investigating principles. In this way I sometimes think that ministers, or they who have been ministers and who have to watch ministers from the Opposition benches, have less opportunity of becoming real politicians than the men who sit in Parliament with empty hands and with time at their own disposal.
    ANTHONY TROLLOPE
    The Prime Minister, 1876

Politicians always do in a crisis what they should have done in the previous crisis.

> DAVID NOBBS
> *Pratt of The Argus*, 1988

That insidious and crafty animal, vulgarly called a statesman or politician, whose councils are directed by momentary fluctuations or affairs.

> ADAM SMITH

A statesman is a politician who places himself at the service of the nation. A politician is a statesman who places the nation at his service.

> GEORGES POMPIDOU, French President 1969-74

A politician is someone with whose politics you don't agree; if you agree with him he is a statesman.

> DAVID LLOYD GEORGE (1863-1945)

The politician is an acrobat. He keeps his balance by saying the opposite of what he does.

MAURICE BARRÈS

Every politician is emphatically a promising politician.

G.K. CHESTERTON

There are some politicians who, if their constituents were cannibals, would promise them missionaries for dinner.

H.L. MENCKEN

Anyone who says he isn't going to resign, four times, definitely will.

J.K. GALBRAITH

In England a man who can't talk morality twice a week to a large, popular, immoral audience is quite over as a serious politician.

OSCAR WILDE
An Ideal Husband, 1895

An attitude of permanent indignation signifies great mental poverty. Politics compels its votaries to take that line and you can see their minds growing more and more impoverished every day, from one burst of righteous anger to the next.

PAUL VALÉRY
Tel Quel, 1943

Your Representative owes you not his industry only, but his judgement; and he betrays instead of serving you if he sacrifices it to your opinion.

EDMUND BURKE
in a speech to the Electors of Bristol, 1774

Practical men, who believe themselves to be quite exempt from any intellectual influences, are usually the slaves of some defunct economist. Madmen in authority, who hear voices in the air, are distilling their frenzy from some academic scribbler of a few years back.

JOHN MAYNARD KEYNES
General Theory of Employment, Interest and Money,
1936

I know a man who used to say,
Not once but twenty times a day,
That in the turmoil and the strife
(His very words) of Public Life
The thing of ultimate effect
Was character – not intellect.

HILAIRE BELLOC
'The Statesman' from *Ladies and Gentlemen*

And order papers were thrown around …

ESSENCE OF PARLIAMENT.
Extracted from the Diary of TOBY, M.P.

House of Commons, Monday, August, 19.—As many pages of this Diary bear record, I have profound respect and admiration for JOSEPH GILLIS. His simplicity of character, his directness of purpose, his genial bearing, his enlightened mind, and his oratorical gifts ever attract me. JOEY B., as was written long ago, is sly—dev'lish sly. No use impecunious member of the community whose financial interests are entrusted to his care coming round him with pleas about drawing a month's, or even a week's, salary in advance. JOSEPH, without causing wing of friendship to moult a feather, ever understands their blandishments. He knows what he's about, and generally accomplishes his end, performing the maximum of public good with the minimum of personal estrangement.

To-day JOSEPH shines in new and brighter light. BALFOUR, desirous of mixing little treacle with the brimstone usually administered to Irish Members, brought in series of Bills appropriating Imperial funds for local works in Ireland. Irish Light Railways Bill one of group. Proposes to advance over half a million sterling towards cost of Irish

He knows nothing and thinks he knows everything. That points clearly to a political career.
> BERNARD SHAW
> *Major Barbara*

He (Prince Metternich) told me that it had been proved in Paris that gambling and politics were the principle causes of suicide. He added that many minds became unhinged in consequence of attending the debates.
> *The Life of Prince Metternich*

Men enter local politics solely as a result of being unhappily married.
> C. NORTHCOTE PARKINSON
> *Parkinson's Law*

To Deptford, reading by the way a most ridiculous play, a new one, called 'The Politician cheated'.
> SAMUEL PEPYS
> *Diary*, 29 July 1663

I am not a politician, and my other habits are good.
> ARTEMUS WARD
> *Fourth of July Oration*

Party is a body of men united, for promoting by their joint endeavours the national interest, upon some particular principle in which they are all agreed.
> EDMUND BURKE
> *Thoughts on the cause of the Present Discontents*, 1770

I don't need fellows to support me when I'm right. I need fellows who support me when I'm wrong.

    LORD MELBOURNE

In politics as on the sickbed people toss from one side to the other thinking they will be more comfortable.

    GOETHE

Party-spirit, which at best is but the madness of many for the gain of a few.

    ALEXANDER POPE

Cease being the slave of a party and you become its deserter.

    JULES SIMON (1814-96)

Some men change their Party for the sake of their principles; others change their principles for the sake of their Party.

    SIR WINSTON CHURCHILL, 1906

Party honesty is party expediency.

    GROVER CLEVELAND, 1889

Do you think that party abuse and the running down of authors is anything new? Look at the manner in which Pope and Dryden were assailed by a set of reptiles. Do you believe that *John Bull* and *Blackwood* had not their prototypes in the party publications of that day? Depend on it, what you take for political cabal and hostility is (nine parts in ten) private pique and malice oozing through those authorized channels.

    JAMES NORTHCOTE (1746-1831)

In every party there is someone who, by his over-devout expression of party principles, provokes the rest to defect.
    NIETZSCHE

There is no act of treachery or mean-ness of which a political party is not capable; for in politics there is no honour.
    BENJAMIN DISRAELI
    Vivien Gray, 1824

The radical invents the views. When he has worn them out, the conservative adopts them.

MARK TWAIN

A radical is a man with both feet planted firmly in the air. A reactionary is a somnambulist walking backwards. A conservative is a man with two perfectly good legs who, however, has never learned how to walk forward. A liberal is a man who uses his legs and his hands at the behest of his head.

FRANKLIN D. ROOSEVELT, 32nd President of the
United States

There are few positions less inspiriting than those of a discomfited party.

BENJAMIN DISRAELI

When in that House MPs divide,
If they've a brain and cerebellum, too,
They've got to leave that brain outside,
And vote just as their leaders tell 'em to.
But then the prospect of a lot
Of dull MPs in close proximity,
All thinking for themselves, is what
No man can face with equanimity.
Then let's rejoice with loud Fal la – Fal lal la!
That nature always does contrive – Fal lal la!
That every boy and every gal
That's born into the world alive
Is either a little Liberal
Or else a little Conservative.

W.S. GILBERT
Iolanthe, 1882

Conservative, n. A statesman who is enamoured of existing evils, as distinguished from the Liberal, who wishes to replace them with others.

> AMBROSE BIERCE
> *The Devil's Dictionary*

'A sound Conservative government', said Taper musingly. 'I understand: Tory men and Whig measures.'

> BENJAMIN DISRAELI
> *Coningsby*, 1844

He thinks like a Tory, and talks like a Radical, and that's so important nowadays.

> OSCAR WILDE
> *Lady Windermere's Fan*, 1892

Why do you talk of Conservatives? A Conservative is only a Tory who is ashamed of himself.

> JOHN HOOKHAM FRERE (1769-1846)

Conservatism is the adherence to the old and tried, against the new and untried.

> ABRAHAM LINCOLN

Conservatives are not necessarily stupid but most stupid people are conservatives.

> JOHN STUART MILL

He who said that all Conservatives are stupid did not know them. Stupid Conservatives there may be, and there certainly are very stupid radicals. The well-educated, widely-read Conservative, who is well assured that all good

things are gradually being brought to an end by the voice of
the people, is generally the pleasantest man to be met.
>ANTHONY TROLLOPE
>*The Eustace Diamonds*, 1873

Liberalism is the trust of the people tempered by prudence;
Conservatism is the distrust of the people tempered by fear.
>WILLIAM GLADSTONE

Though I believe in liberalism I find it difficult to believe in
Liberals.
>G.K. CHESTERTON

A respectable vague liberalism, though it often disappears
with the first grey hair, marriage, and professional success,
does nevertheless raise a man's character.
>ALEXANDER HERZEN (1812-70)

The inherent virtue of Socialism is the equal sharing of
miseries.
>SIR WINSTON CHURCHILL
>in a speech in the House of Commons, 22 October
>1945

I criticize doctrinaire State Socialism because it is, in fact,
little better than a dusty survival of a plan to meet the
problems of fifty years ago, based on a misunderstanding of
what someone said a hundred years ago.
>JOHN MAYNARD KEYNES

Socialism is workable only in heaven, where it isn't
needed, and in hell, where they've got it.
>CECIL PALMER

A man who is not something of a socialist before he is forty has no heart. Any man who is still a socialist after he is forty has no head.
>WENDEL L. WILKIE

The function of socialism is to raise suffering to a higher level.
>NORMAN MAILER

What is a Communist? One who has yearnings
For equal division of unequal earnings.
>EBENEZER ELLIOTT
>*Epigrams*

Anyone who deliberately tries to get himself elected to public office is permanently disqualified from holding one.
>SIR THOMAS MORE
>*Utopia*, 1516

If you would know the depth of meanness of human nature, you have got to be a prime minister running a general election.
>JOHN A MACDONALD, first Prime Minister of Canada, 1867

Bad officials are elected by good citizens who do not vote.
>GEORGE JEAN NATHAN

People on whom I do not bother to dote
Are people who do not bother to vote.
Heaven forbid they should ever be exempt
From contumely, obloquy and various kinds of
    contempt.
OGDEN NASH
'Election Day is a Holiday', *Happy Days*, 1933

To compare Carlingford to a volcano that night (and
indeed all the next day, which was the day of nomination)
would be a stale similitude; and yet in some respects it was
like a volcano. It was not the same kind of excitement
which arises in a town where politics run very high – if
there are any towns nowadays in such a state of
unsophisticated nature. Neither was it a place where simple
corruption could carry the day; for the freemen of
Wharfside were, after all, but a small portion of the
population. It was in reality a quite ideal sort of contest – a
contest for the best man, such as would have pleased the
purest-minded philosopher. It was the man most fit to
represent Carlingford for whom everybody was looking, not
a man to be baited about parish-rates and Reform Bills and
the Irish Church; – a man who lived in, or near the town,
and 'dealt regular' at all the best shops; a man who would
not disgrace his constituency by any unlawful or injudicious
sort of love-making – who would attend to the town's
interests and subscribe to its charities, and take the lead in
a general way. This was what Carlingford was looking for,
as Miss Marjoribanks, with that intuitive rapidity which
was characteristic of her genius, had at once remarked ...
MRS OLIPHANT
Miss Marjoribanks, 1866

Elections are a moral horror, as bad as a battleground except for the blood; a mud bath for every soul concerned in it.

    BERNARD SHAW

People never lie so much as after a hunt, during a war or before an election.

    OTTO VON BISMARCK

Parliamentary canvassing is not a pleasant occupation. Perhaps nothing more disagreeable, more squalid, more revolting to the senses, more opposed to personal dignity, can be conceived. The same words have to be repeated over and over again in the cottages, hovels, and lodgings of poor men and women who only understand that the time has come round in which they are to be flattered instead of being the flatterers. 'I think I am right in supposing that your husband's principles are Conservative, Mrs Bubbs.' 'I don't know nothing about it. You'd better call again and see Bubbs hissel.' 'Certainly I will do so. I shouldn't at all like to leave the borough without seeing Mr Bubbs. I hope we shall have your influence, Mrs Bubbs.' ... Such is the conversation in which the candidate takes a part, while his cortege at the door is criticising his very imperfect mode of securing Mrs Bubbs' good wishes. Then he goes on to the next house, and the same thing, with some variation, is endured again ... It is a nuisance in any weather. But when it rains there is superadded a squalor and an ill humour to all the party which makes it almost impossible for them not to quarrel before the day is over. To talk politics to Mrs Bubbs in any circumstances is bad, but to do so with the conviction that the moisture is penetrating from your great-coat through your shirt to your bones, and that while

so employed you are breathing the steam from those seven other wet men at the door, is abominable.
ANTHONY TROLLOPE
The Duke's Children, 1880

The real object is to vote for a good politician, not for the kind-hearted or agreeable man: the mischief is just the same to the country whether I am smiled into a corrupt choice or frowned into a corrupt choice.
SYDNEY SMITH (1771-1845)

An election is like a violent love affair.
HENRY 'CHIPS' CHANNON
Diary, 1951

The English people imagine themselves to be free, but they are wrong: it is only during the election of members of Parliament that they are so.
JEAN-JACQUES ROUSSEAU
Contrat Social, 1762

When political columnists say 'Every thinking man' they mean themselves; and when the candidates appeal to 'every intelligent worker', they mean everybody who is going to vote for them.
FRANKLIN P. ADAMS (1881-1960)

In politics women type the letters, lick the stamps, distribute the pamphlets and get out the vote. Men get elected.
CLARE BOOTHE LUCE

When a child of tender age,
I'd a monkey in a cage.
Now I have no need for pets,
Mother's joined the Suffragettes.
>   HARRY GRAHAM
>   *Ruthless Rhymes for Heartless Homes*

I was introduced by Mr Balfour and Mr Lloyd George, men who had always been in favour of votes for women. But when I walked up the aisle of the House of Commons I felt they were more nervous than I was, for I was deeply conscious of representing a *Cause*, whereas I think they were a little nervous of having let down the House of Commons by escorting the *Cause* into it.
>   NANCY ASTOR, first woman to take her seat in the
>   House of Commons, in 1919
>   in a BBC radio broadcast, October 1943

To introduce ... women into a male assembly is to introduce an element of confusion ... The whole process of putting minds together into a common pool so that a corporate judgment may be formed is disturbed and confused ... Agreement between a man and a woman or disagreement between a man and a woman are different things from agreement and disagreement between two men or between two women. They are complicated by the inevitable influence of sex ... For myself therefore, notwithstanding the interesting personality of the new member, I regret the result of the Plymouth election, and I earnestly hope no other constituency will follow the example of Plymouth.
>   LORD HUGH CECIL MP
>   'Women in Parliament', *Pall Mall Gazette*, 1919

Under the old bribery laws, an artful fellow contrived the following cheap and safe trick for getting into Parliament as the representative of a cheap borough. At an election there, prior to the occasion on which he calculated that his object would be accomplished, he presented himself as a candidate, and making no promises or presents obtained, as he had expected, very few suppoorters. With these few, however, numbering some half-dozen, he went to the poll, and shortly afterwards sent a handsome amount of head-money to each of them. This was soon noised abroad, and produced the expected effect upon the electoral mind throughout the borough. At the general election he reappeared, was received with universal acclamation, and came in at the head of the poll without giving or promising sixpence. The head-money was naturally expected as before, but this expectation was never realized. Of course, the honourable member could never show his face again in that borough; but at least he had been a member in one parliament, without danger and without costs.

LORD ELDON (1751-1838)

I know I am popular, and my majority last time of only 3,077 should be greatly increased. It is lonely in Southend by myself. I wish I had a black poodle puppy as a companion, in fact I wish I had many things, but first and foremost a safe majority.

HENRY 'CHIPS' CHANNON
Diary, 1951

No part of the education of a politician is more indispensable than the fighting of elections.

SIR WINSTON CHURCHILL
Great Contemporaries

It is something to have sat in the House of Commons, though it has been for one session! ... England does not choose her six hundred and fifty four best men. One comforts one's self, sometimes, with remembering that ... Dishonesty, ignorance and vulgarity do not close the gate of that heaven against aspirants; ... But though England does not send thither none but her best men, the best of her commoners do find their way there. It is the highest and most legitimate pride of an Englishman to have the letters MP written after his name. No selection from the alphabet, no fellowship, be it of ever so learned or royal a society, no knightship, – not though it be of the Garter, – confers so fair an honour.

> ANTHONY TROLLOPE
> *Can You Forgive Her?*, 1864

Only people who look dull ever get into the House of Commons, and only people who are dull ever succeed there.

> OSCAR WILDE
> *An Ideal Husband*

You will not make love! You will not intrigue! You have your seat; do not risk anything! If you meet with a widow, then marry.

> COUNT D'ORSAY to Benjamin Disraeli

To the young members who have just come I would say that for the first six months after you are here you will wonder how you got here. Then after that you will wonder how the rest of the members ever got here.

> JOHN DIEFENBAKER, addressing a newly elected
> Canadian Parliament

Opposition, n. In politics the party that prevents the Government from running amuck by hamstringing it.

    AMBROSE BIERCE
    The Devil's Dictionary

England does not love coalitions.

    BENJAMIN DISRAELI
    in a speech in the House of Commons, 1852

For those who govern, the first thing required is indifference to newspapers.
LOUIS THIERS (1797-1877)

The first mistake in public business is the going into it.
BENJAMIN FRANKLIN

Our opposition parties seldom form a regular battalion. Even the leaders often have detached views. To form a firm array, even the common soldiers should be valued by the chiefs, and have their encouragements and rewards. The scaffolding is neglected after the house is built, but the necks of the builders may be hazarded by neglecting it before.
HORACE WALPOLE (1718-97)

When I first came into Parliament, Mr Tierney, a great Whig authority, used always to say that the duty of an Opposition was very simple – it was to oppose everything and propose nothing.
LORD STANLEY
Hansard, 4 June 1841

No government can be long secure without a formidable opposition.
BENJAMIN DISRAELI

All political parties die at last of swallowing their own lies.
attributed to JOHN ARBUTHNOT
Life of Emerson

I can assure the Right Hon. Gentleman [Herbert Morrison] that the spectacle of a number of middle-aged gentlemen who are my political opponents being in a state of uproar and fury is really quite exhilarating to me.

SIR WINSTON CHURCHILL
Hansard, 21 May 1952

By the time that the Easter holidays were over, – holidays that had been used do conveniently for the making of a new government, – the work of getting a team together had been accomplished by the united energy of the two dukes and other friends ... *Noblesse Oblige*. The Secretaries of State, and the Chancellors, and the First Lords, selected from this or the other party, felt the eyes of mankind were upon them, and that it behoved them to assume a virtue if they had it not ... professing that the Queen's Government and the good of the country were their only considerations ... And Sir Gregory Grogram said not a word, whatever he may have thought, when he was told that Mr Daubeny's Lord Chancellor, Lord Ramsden, was to keep the seals. Sir Gregory did, no doubt, think very much about it; for legal offices have a signification differing much from that which attaches itself to places simply political. A Lord Chancellor becomes a peer, and on going out of office enjoys a large pension. When the woolsack has been reached there comes an end of doubt, and a beginning of ease. Sir Gregory was not a young man, and this was a terrible blow. But he bore it manfully, saying not a word when the Duke spoke to him; but he became convinced from that moment that no more

inefficient lawyer ever sat upon the English bench, or a
more presumptuous politician in the British Parliament,
than Lord Ramsden.

ANTHONY TROLLOPE
The Prime Minister, 1876

In this House, which is termed a place of free speech, there
is nothing so necessary for the preservation of the prince
and State as free speech; and without this it is a scorn and
mockery to call it a Parliament House, for in truth it is
none but a very school of flattery and dissimulation, and so
a fit place to serve the devil and his angels in, and not to
glorify God and benefit the Commonwealth.

PETER WENTWORTH
in a speech in the House of Commons, 8 February
1576

Mr Donne from London with letters that tell us the
welcome news of the Parliament's votes yesterday, which
will be remembered for the happiest May-day that hath
been many a year to England. The king's letter was read in
the House; wherein he submits himself and all things to
them, as an Act of Oblivion to all, unless they shall please
to except any, as to the confirming of the sales of the King's
and Church lands, if they see good. The House, upon
reading the letter, ordered 50,000l. to be forthwith
provided to send to his Majesty for his present supply; and a
committee chosen to return an answer of thanks to His
Majesty for his gracious letter and that the letter be kept
among the records of the Parliament; and in all this not so
much as one No.

SAMUEL PEPYS
Diary, 2 May 1660

By water to Westminster, and there come most luckily to
the Lords' House, as the House of Commons was going into
the Lords' House, and there I crowded in along with the
Speaker, and got to stand close behind him, where he made
his speech to the King (who sat with his crown on and
robes, and so all the Lords in their robes, a fine sight);
wherein he told his Majesty what they have done this
Parliament, and now offered for his royall consent. The
greatest matters were a bill for the Lord's day (which it
seems the Lords have lost, and so cannot be passed, at
which the Commons are displeased.) The bills against
conventicles and Papists (but it seems the Lords have not
passed them), and giving his Majesty four entire subsidys;
which last, with about twenty smaller Acts, were passed
with this form: The Clerk of the House reads the title of the
bill, and then looks at the end and there finds (writ by the
King I suppose) 'Le Roy le veult', and that he reads.

> SAMUEL PEPYS
> *Diary*, 27 July 1663

Great high words in the House on Saturday last upon the
first part of the Committee's Report about the dividing of
the fleet; wherein some would have the counsels of the
King to be declared, and the reasons of them, and who did
give them; where Sir W. Coventry laid open to them the
consequences of doing that, that, the King would never
have any honest and wise men ever to be of his Council.
They did here in the House talk boldly of the King's bad
Counsellors, and how they must all be turned out, and
many others, and better brought in: and the proceedings of

the Long Parliament in the beginning of the war were called to memory.

SAMUEL PEPYS
Diary, 17 February 1668

The members of the House of Commons have nothing particular about their dress; they even come into the house in their great coats, and with boots and spurs. It is not at all uncommon to see a member lying stretched out on one of the benches, while others are debating. Some crack nuts, others eat oranges, or what-ever else is in season. There is no end to their going in and out; and as often as anyone wishes to go out, he places himself before the speaker, and makes him a bow, as if, like a schoolboy, he asked his tutor's permission ... If it happens that a member rises, who is but a bad speaker, or if what he says is generally deemed not sufficiently interesting, so much noise is made, that he can scarcely distinguish his own words ... On the contrary, when a favourite member, and one who speaks well, and to the purpose, rises, the most perfect silence reigns: and his friends and admirers, one after another, make their approbation known by calling out 'Hear him' ...

C.P. MORITZ
Travels in England in 1782

I went with my father several times to the House of Commons and what creatures did I see there! What faces! What an expression of countenance! What wretched beings! Good God! what men did we meet about the House! in the lobbies and passages! and my father was so civil to all of them – to animals that I regarded with unmitigated disgust.

PERCY BYSSHE SHELLEY

No man is regular in his attendance at the House of Commons until he is married.
BENJAMIN DISRAELI
Vivian Grey, 1824

We are provincial, because we do not find at home our standards; because we do not worship truth but the reflection of truth; because we are warped and narrowed by an exclusive devotion to trade and commerce and manufactures and agriculture and the like, which are but means, and not the end. So is the English parliament provincial. Mere country bumpkins they betray themselves, when any more important question arises for them to settle … Their natures are subdued to what they work in … They appear but as the fashions of past days – mere courtliness, knee buckles and smallclothes, out of date … they are cast-off clothes or shells, claiming the respect which belonged to the living creature.

> HENRY DAVID THOREAU
> 'Life Without Principle', *Atlantic Monthly*, October 1863

There is hardly a single person in the House of Commons worth painting; though many of them would be better for a little whitewashing.

> OSCAR WILDE
> *The Picture of Dorian Gray*

Westminster politicians in 1906, as seen by *Punch*

The House of Commons is a mixed body. I except the minority, which I hold to be pure; but I take the whole House. It is a mass by no means pure; but neither is it wholly corrupt, though there is a large proportion of corruption in it.

    EDMUND BURKE

No one enjoys the House of Commons more than I. I am truly bitten by it. I like the male society. It reminds me of Oxford or perhaps of the private school to which I never went.

    HENRY 'CHIPS' CHANNON
    Diary, 1946

It's not so much a gentleman's club as a boy's boarding school.

    SHIRLEY WILLIAMS

It is very worthwhile for a man to speak well in Parliament. A man who has vanity speaks to display his talents; and if a man speaks well he gradually establishes a certain reputation and consequence in the general opinion, which sooner or later will have its reward. Besides, though not one vote is gained, a good speech has its effect.

    EDMUND BURKE

Early on that same day Faringcourt had spoken in the House, – a man to whom no one would lend a shilling, whom the privilege of that House kept out of gaol, whose word no man believed; who was wifeless, childless, and unloved. But three hundred men had hung listening upon his words. When he laughed in his speech, they laughed; when he was indignant against the Minister, they sat breathless, as the Spaniard sits in the critical moment of the bull killing. Whichever way he turned himself, he carried them with him. Crowds of Members flocked into the House from libraries and smoking-rooms when it was known that this ne're do well was on his legs. The Strangers' Gallery was filled to overflowing. The reporters turned their rapid pages, working their fingers wearily till the sweat drops stood upon their brows. And as the Premier was attacked with some special impetus of redoubled irony, men declared that he would be driven to enrol the speaker among his colleagues, in spite of dishonoured bills and evil reports. A man who could shake thunderbolts like that must be paid to shake them on the right side.

ANTHONY TROLLOPE
Can You Forgive Her?, 1864

Now it was probably not in the remembrance of any gentleman there that a member had got up to make a speech within two or three hours of his first entry into the House ... As soon as Melmotte was on his legs, and, looking round, found that everybody was silent with the intent of listening to him, a good deal of his courage oozed out of his fingers' ends. The House, which, to his thinking, had by no means been august while Mr Brown had been toddling through his speech, now became awful. He caught the eyes of great men fixed upon him, – of men who had not seemed to him to be at all great as he had watched them a few minutes before, yawning beneath their hats. Mr Brown, poor as his speech had been, had, no doubt, prepared it, – and had perhaps made three or four such speeches every year for the last fifteen years. Melmotte had not dreamed of putting two words together. He had thought, as far as he had thought at all, that he could rattle off what he had to say just as he might do it when seated in his chair at the Mexican Railway Board. But there was the Speaker, and those three clerks in their wigs, and the mace, – and worse than all, the eyes of that long row of statesmen opposite to him! His position was felt by him to be dreadful. He had forgotten even the very point on which he had intended to crush Mr Brown.

ANTHONY TROLLOPE
The Way We Live Now, 1875

A stranger erupting into the Peers' Gallery

He can best be described as one of those orators who, before they get up, do not know what they are going to say; when they are speaking, do not know what they are saying; and when they have sat down, do not know what they have said.

SIR WINSTON CHURCHILL on Lord Charles Beresford in 1911

That this House recognizes that for a speech to be immortal it does not have to be eternal and that the standard of debate would be greatly improved if all back-bench speeches were limited to 15 minutes and all front-bench speeches to 30 minutes without the specific permission of the House.

Early Day Motion No. 817, 21 June 1984

Most of the day at the House of Commons. Today for the first time I really liked it; boredom passed and a glow of pleasure filtered through me. But I wish I understood what I was voting for.

HENRY 'CHIPS' CHANNON
Diary, 1936

'Go down to the House at two o'clock, indeed! It would give me no time for luncheon … I shall vote against that!'

I grew so rich that I was sent
By a pocket borough into Parliament.
I always voted at my party's call,
And I never thought of thinking for myself at all.
I thought so little they rewarded me
By making me the Ruler of the Queen's Navee!
W.S. GILBERT
H.M.S. Pinafore, 1878

My only great qualification for being put in charge of the Navy is that I am very much at sea.

> EDWARD CARSON, 1916

I slept for two hours this afternoon in the Library of the House of Commons! A deep House of Commons sleep. There is no sleep to compare with it – rich, deep and guilty.

> HENRY 'CHIPS' CHANNON
> *Diary*, 1939

The Commons, faithful to their system, remained in a wise and masterly inactivity.

> SIR JAMES MACKINTOSH
> *Vindiciae Gallicae*

Ye supple MPs, who go down on your knees,
Your precious identity sinking,
And vote black or white as your leaders indite
(Which saves you the trouble of thinking),
For your country's good fame, her repute, or her shame,
You don't care the snuff of a candle –
But you're paid for your game when you're told that your
    name
Will be graced by a baronet's handle –
Oh! allow me to give *you* a word of advice –
The title's uncommonly dear at the price!

> W.S. GILBERT
> *Ruddigore*, 1887

The cure for admiring the House of Lords is to go and look at it.

> WALTER BAGEHOT

Kelvil: May I ask, Lord Illingworth, if you regard the House of Lords as a better institution than the House of Commons?

Lord Illingworth: A much better institution of course. We in the House of Lords are never in touch with public opinion. That makes us a civilized body.

> OSCAR WILDE
> *A Woman of No Importance*, 1893

A fully equipped Duke costs as much to keep as two Dreadnoughts, and they are just as great a terror – and they last longer.

> DAVID LLOYD GEORGE
> in a speech in Newcastle, 9 October 1909

What I like about the Garter is that there is no damned merit about it.

> attributed to LORD MELBOURNE

Chorus of Peers: 'Suppose we can't help this thing passing –
but oh, the vibration!' (1906 *Punch* cartoon)

When Britain ruled the waves –
(In good Queen Bess's time)
The House of Peers made no pretence
To intellectual eminence,
Or scholarship sublime;
Yet Britain won her proudest bays
In good Queen Bess's glorious days!

When Wellington thrashed Bonaparte,
As every child can tell,
The House of Peers, throughout the war,
Did nothing in particular,
And did it very well:
Yet Britain set the world ablaze
In good King George's glorious days!

And while the House of Peers withholds
Its legislative hand,
And noble statesmen do not itch
To interfere with matters which
They do not understand,
As bright will shine Great Britain's rays
As in King George's glorious days!
    W.S. GILBERT
    Iolanthe, 1882

The Choice of a Leader
    The Recess nearly spent, and approaching the hour,
    That renews the vain struggle for places and power,
    The Whigs, duly summon'd, are met to prepare
    Their annual bill of political fare.
    …
    Let us see what is chiefly required in a Leader?

Not the fire of a bully, the phlegm of a pleader:
Not a blusterer 'tearing a passion to rags';
Not one who at nothing laboriously fags,
But sound common sense, quiet, pliant, and cool;
An address – which can work with a fact like a tool;
A conscience – not qualmish, nor apt to grow sick;
An art – as plain dealing to pass off a trick:
To these, with a plausible manner and face,
My scheme for a Leader assigns the first place.

The next proposition I mean to advance
Is this – that our chief should be skilled in finance:
Can one, not expert at financial debate,
To any extent clog the wheels of the State?
What hope have we left but to bare to the axe
That root of exertion the Property Tax?
This done, a wise chief might proceed to assault
The Excise and the Customs, the Land and the Malt;
And then it might be to the country revealed
That taxes are needless, and should be repealed;
And that, by disbanding the Army and Fleet,
Economical Statesmen might make both ends meet.
For my part I'll vote for no leader alive
Who cannot explain two and two to make five.

My third and last point I now hasten to state:
No leader can properly guide a debate
Unless quite familiar with everyone's views.
He sees the whole game which each party pursues;
And knows who are nibbling, who hungry, who nice –
The hope of each faction – and every man's price!
  ANON., 1815, published in *The New Whig Guide*,
  1824

The first essential for a Prime Minister is to be a good butcher.

> WILLIAM GLADSTONE
> quoted in *Great Contemporaries* by Winston Churchill

I have lived long enough in the world to know that the safety of a minister lies in his having the approbation of this House. Former ministers, Sir, neglected this and therefore they fell; I have always made it my first study to obtain it, and therefore I hope to stand.

> SIR ROBERT WALPOLE
> in a speech in the House of Commons, 21 November 1739

William Pitt has not only the most extraordinary talents, but appears to be immediately gifted by nature with the judgment which others acquire by experience. Though judgment is not so rare in youth as is generally supposed, I have commonly observed that those who do not possess it early are apt to miss it late.

> EDMUND BURKE on William Pitt the Younger

People little knew what he [William Pitt the Younger] had to do. Up at eight in the morning, with people enough to see for a week, obliged to talk all the time he was at breakfast, and receiving first one, then another, until four o'clock; then eating a mutton-chop, hurrying off to the House, and there badgered and compelled to speak and waste his lungs until two or three in the morning! – who could stand it? After this, heated as he was, and having eaten nothing, in a manner of speaking, all day, he would sup with Dundas, Huskisson, Rose, Mr Long, and such persons, and then go to bed to get three or four hours sleep, and to renew the same thing the next day, and the next, and the next ...

LADY HESTER STANHOPE
Memoirs of the Lady Hester Stanhope, 1846

Mr Canning's death will not do all the good it might have done at a later period. But it is still a great public advantage.

THE DUKE OF WELLINGTON, 1827

I would rather my husband was only Foreign Minister or Home Secretary, for since he became Prime Minister I see nothing of him. He never comes to bed till four or five o'clock.

LADY PALMERSTON

A sophistical rhetorician inebriated with the exuberance of his own verbosity.

DISRAELI on Gladstone

He did not object, he once said, to Gladstone's always having the ace of trumps up his sleeve, but only to his pretence that God had put it there.

HENRY LABOUCHERE (1831-1912)
opinion of Gladstone, quoted in the *Dictionary of National Biography*

If Gladstone fell into the Thames, that would be a misfortune. And if anyone pulled him out, that, I suppose, would be a calamity.

BENJAMIN DISRAELI, when asked to distinguish between misfortune and calamity

Gladstone setting out on a trip to the Baltic in June 1895,
as seen by *Punch*

There are two supreme pleasures in life. One is ideal, the other real. The ideal is when a man receives the office from his Sovereign. The real pleasure comes when he hands it back.

LORD ROSEBERY

Nothing matters very much, and very few things matter at all.

ARTHUR BALFOUR

Mr Balfour was difficult to understand ... and difficult to know intimately because of his formidable detachment. The most that many of us could hope for was that he had a taste in us as one might have in clocks or china.

MARGOT ASQUITH
Autobiography, 1962

Personally I am a great believer in bed, in constantly keeping horizontal ... the heart and everything else go slower, and the whole system is refreshed.

HENRY CAMPBELL-BANNERMAN

Count not his broken pledges as a crime
He MEANT them, HOW he meant them – at the time.
KENSAL GREEN on Lloyd George

Asquith when drunk can make a better speech than any of us when sober.

ANDREW BONAR LAW

Of all the politicians I ever saw
The least significant was Bonar Law.
Unless it was MacDonald by the way:
Or Baldwin – it's impossible to say.
HILAIRE BELLOC

If God were to come to me and say, 'Ramsay, would you rather be a country gentleman than a Prime Minister?', I should reply, 'Please God, a country gentleman'.

> RAMSAY MACDONALD, 5 October 1930
> quoted in Harold Nicolson's *Diaries and Letters 1930-39*

The furnace of war has smelted out all base metals from him.

> STANLEY BALDWIN on Winston Churchill, 1943

I have nothing to offer but blood, tears and sweat.

> WINSTON CHURCHILL
> in a speech in the House of Commons, 13 May 1940

There are two problems in my life. The political ones are insoluble and the economic ones are incomprehensible.

> ALEC DOUGLAS-HOME

She has eyes like Caligula and the mouth of Marilyn Monroe.

> FRANÇOIS MITTERRAND on Margaret Thatcher

Ladies and Gentlemen, I stand before you tonight in my green chiffon evening gown, my face softly made up, my fair hair gently waved ... The Iron Lady of the Western World. Me?

> MARGARET THATCHER, 31 January 1976

Mabel Chiltern: Oh! I hope you are not going to leave me all alone with Lord Goring? Especially at such an early hour in the day.

Lord Caversham: I am afraid I can't take him with me to Downing Street. It is not the Prime Minister's day for seeing the unemployed.

> OSCAR WILDE
> *An Ideal Husband*, 1895

Some little political trouble I imagine. Politics in Turkey are taken more seriously than they are at home. It was only recently that they executed a Prime Minister. We dream of it, they act.

> GRAHAM GREENE
> *Travels With My Aunt*, 1969

... where Princes grew indolent and careless of their own affairs through a constant love and pursuit of pleasure, they made use of such an administrator as I had mentioned, under the title of first or chief Minister of State, the description of which ... may be allowed to be as follows: That he is a person wholly exempt from joy or grief, love and hatred, pity and anger – at least, makes use of no other passions but a violent desire of wealth, power, and titles; that he never tells words to all uses except to the indication of his mind; that he never tells a truth but with an intent that you should take it for a lie, nor a lie but with a design that you should take it for a truth; that those he speaks worst of behind their backs are in the surest way to preferment, and whenever he begins to praise you to others or to yourself, you are from that day forlorn.

> JONATHAN SWIFT
> *Gulliver's Travels*, A Voyage to the Country of the Houyhnhnms, 1726

Yesterday the greatest question was decided which was ever debated in America; and a greater perhaps never was, nor will be, decided among men. A resolution was passed without one dissenting colony, that those United Colonies are, and of right ought to be, free and independent States.

> JOHN ADAMS
> in a letter to Mrs Adams, 3 July 1776

The manners of women are the surest criterion by which to determine whether a republican government is practicable in a nation or not.

> JOHN ADAMS
> *Diary*, 2 June 1778

The Republican form of Government is the highest form of government; but because of this it requires the highest type of human nature – a type nowhere at present existing.

> HERBERT SPENCER
> essay on *The Americas*, 1891

Well, will anybody deny now that the Government at Washington, as regards its own people, is the strongest government in the world at this hour? And for this simple reason, that it is based on the will, and the good will, of an instructed people.

> JOHN BRIGHT
> *Speech at Rochdale*, 24 November 1863

The men the American people admire most extravagantly are the most daring liars; the men they detest most violently are those who try to tell them the truth. A Galileo could no more be elected President of the United States than he could be elected Pope of Rome. Both high posts are reserved for men favoured by God with an extraordinary genius for swathing the bitter facts of life in bandages of soft illusion.

> H.L. MENCKEN, 1918

He was a man whose soul might be turned wrong side outwards without discovering a blemish to the world.

> THOMAS JEFFERSON on James Monroe, fifth President of the United States

He sailed through American history like a steel ship loaded with monoliths of granite.
> H.L. MENCKEN on Grover Cleveland (1837-1908)
> 22nd and 24th President of the United States

I think the American people wants a solemn ass as a President. And I think I'll go along with them.
> CALVIN COOLIDGE, 30th President of the USA

I've noticed that nothing I've never said has hurt me.
> CALVIN COOLIDGE

It is difficult for men in high office to avoid the malady of self-delusion. They are always surrounded by worshippers. They are constantly, and for the most part sincerely, assured of their greatness.
> CALVIN COOLIDGE

I don't know whether you fellows ever had a load of hay fall on you, but when they told me yesterday what had happened, I felt like the moon, the stars, and all the planets had fallen on me.
> HARRY S. TRUMAN, learning he had become President on Roosevelt's death, 13 April 1945

My fellow Americans, ask not what your country can do for you; ask what you can do for your country. My fellow citizens of the world, ask not what America will do for you, but what together we can do for the freedom of man.

> JOHN F. KENNEDY, 35th President of the United States
> Inaugural Address, 20 January 1961

The Presidency, so fought for by fugitives from the sewers.
> H.L. MENCKEN, 1920

Presidency, n. The greased pig in the field game of American politics.

President, n. The leading figure in a small group of men of whom – and of whom only – it is positively known that immense numbers of their countrymen did not want any of them for President.

Congress, n. A body of men who meet to repeal laws.

Senate, n. A body of elderly gentlemen charged with high duties and misdemeanours.
> AMBROSE BIERCE
> *The Devil's Dictionary*

Reader, suppose you were an idiot; and suppose you were a member of Congress; but I repeat myself.

MARK TWAIN

You can't use tact with a Congressman! A congressman is a hog! You must take a stick and hit him on the snout.

HENRY ADAMS

That one hundred and fifty lawyers should do business together ought not to be expected.

THOMAS JEFFERSON on Congress
Autobiography, 1821

But in this world nothing can be said to be certain, except death and taxes.

BENJAMIN FRANKLIN
in a letter to Jean Baptiste Le Roy, 13 November 1789